BIGFOOT: ANCIENT APE OF THE NORTHWEST

. . . .

ANDREW LAWRENCE

Alphabet Publishing

αβ

www.AlphabetPublish.com

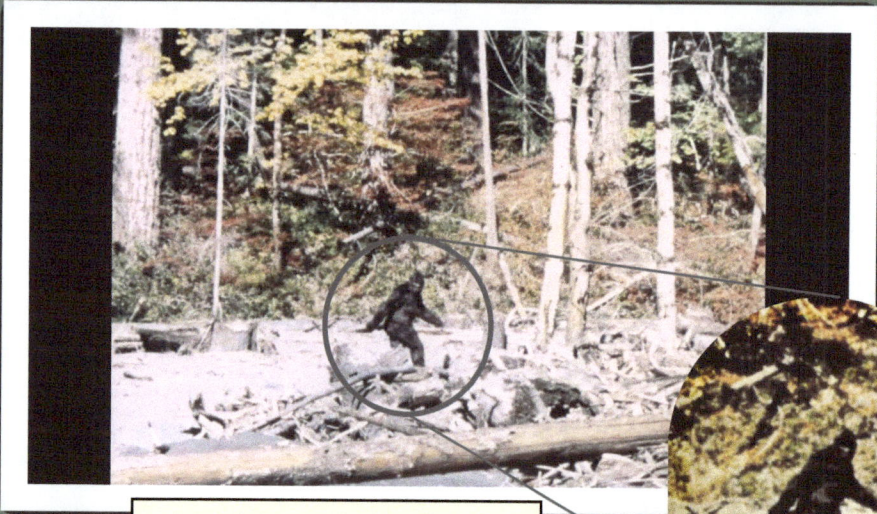

Still and close-up from the
Patterson-Gilman film

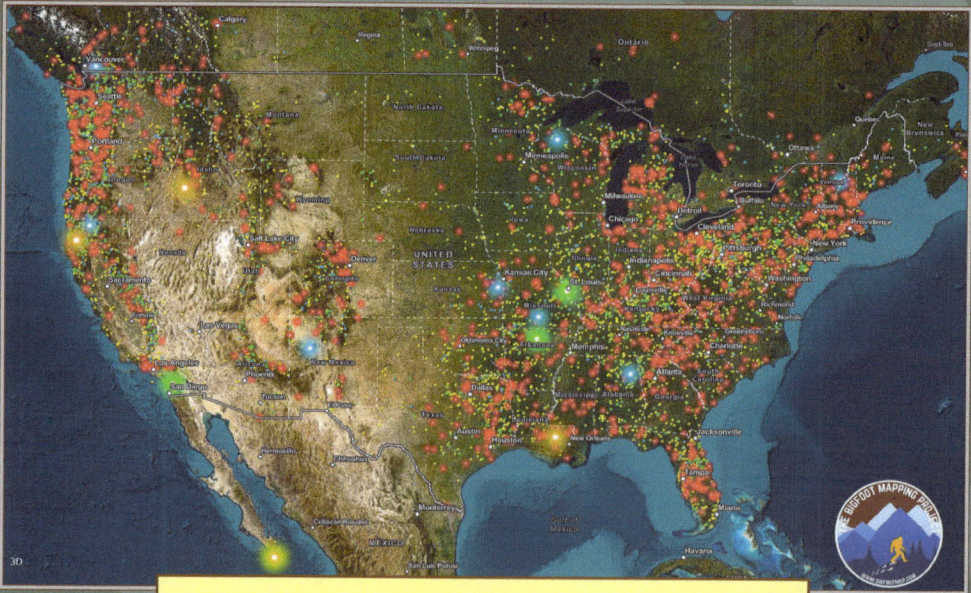

Recent reported Bigfoot sightings
from The Bigfoot Mapping Project

For thousands of years, people have whispered about Bigfoot (also known as Sasquatch), a giant, hairy, ape-like creature who lives secretly in the forests of North America. Are these just legends, or is it possible that there is a mysterious and secretive animal roaming the woods of the Northwest? If so, what new things could this tell us about human history and society?

INTRODUCTION

Is it possible that there are animals left in the world that people just don't know about? The forests of the Western United States of America and Canada are vast, and mostly unexplored and unoccupied. Still, people pass through them all the time, so you would think that we have discovered everything there is in there.

However, stories about Bigfoot persist. Beginning when the first Native Americans came to this land 6,000 years ago, there have been sightings of a hairy, 6- to 9-foot (2- to 3-meter)-tall creature with 24-inch (60-centimeter-)-long feet. Some people say that these are only scary stories that people tell, or that the sightings were just a bear or moose or other large animal. But what if Bigfoot is real?

Many believers think that Bigfoot is a "missing link" between humans and apes, such as gorillas or orangutans. A missing link is a long-ago creature scientists think might explain how one type of animal changed into another. Others think that they may be similar to the Neanderthals, a species very similar to humans that evolved alongside us, but eventually branched off and died out. Still others say that it is a tribe of hairy people that has always lived deep in the mountains and caves.

What do you think? Could a Bigfoot be real? Were they alive in the past, but now extinct? Why have people told stories of seeing them for so long? And what about some of the pictures and videos that people say show Bigfoot?

Read the facts and decide for yourself!

Introductory Questions

1. What do you know about Bigfoot?

2. Do people in your hometown or country ever tell stories about strange creatures?

3. Do you believe any part of these stories? Why or why not?

4. What would you do if you saw a creature like this? Would you tell anyone?

CONTENTS

BEGINNINGS

When did people first come to the American continent? And how did they get there? While some may have come on boats from Europe or Asia, most experts believe that around 20,000 years ago humans first came from Siberia, in the far east of what is now Russia. They used a temporary land bridge to where today's U.S. state of Alaska is located. Because this was during a long, cold time, so much sea water was frozen in glaciers that the level of the oceans was much lower. This made it possible to walk from Asia to North America through an area called Beringia for about 5,000 years, until the glaciers melted again and the oceans rose to where they are today.

Imagine you were one of these ancient travelers: what would you be expecting to find in this new land? Would you even be aware

Lena R.

ARCTIC OCEAN

-120 meters

21,000 BP shoreline

Present-day shoreline

RUSSIA

Mackenzie R.

ARCTIC

B E R I N G I A

Yukon R.

Kolyma R.

Chukchi Pen.

Seward Pen.

CANAD U.S.

Alaska

Kamchatka Peninsula

Gulf of Alaska

Bering Sea

21,000 BP glacial ice

6

0   600 mi

0   600 km

PACIFIC OCEAN

that you were entering a huge place where no people had ever been before? Is it possible that when these people crossed over they found themselves face-to-face with gigantic, hairy, ape-like creatures? When thinking about Bigfoot, known by some native peoples as Sasquatch, we must ask these questions. Why? Because the stories about this creature are not only from the present day, or from when the Europeans arrived in the Northwest some 500 years ago: they have been passed on among native peoples for as long as they have lived on the continent. Why would they tell these stories, unless Bigfoot was real?

No one can doubt that the early people of North America lived among a huge variety of wild animals, such as bears, moose, wolves, and more. Some would be familiar to them. Others might be elusive, or only seen when exploring new areas. In order to make sense of the world around them and to pass on their culture and knowledge to their children, most Native American tribes had a vast oral tradition: stories that they would tell over and over for many generations. Most tribes also did not have a written language, so telling stories—and remembering them—is a major way that they recorded their history and etched it into their memories.

NATIVE STORIES

Across today's U.S. state of Oregon, coastal tribes like the Tillamook connect Bigfoot to legends of "wild men" who lived near villages and left giant footprints. Tribes on the other side of the Cascade Mountains, such as those on the Warm Springs Reservation, saw Bigfoot as a sneaky being who could steal fish or mislead people by whistling or throwing rocks, leaving them lost. The Lummi people, who live today in Washington State around the far western border between the U.S. and Canada, speak of "Ts'emekwes", a race of nocturnal, hairy giants that dwell in the mountains and forests.

That is not to say that there are only stories from native people about this ape-man. Possibly the oldest piece of Bigfoot evidence we have is the cave drawings, or pictographs, of "Mayak Datat", or "Hairy Man", drawn by the Tule People of what is now northern California. According to tribal members, the paintings, which are around 1,000 years old, tell the story of how a group of animals (including Hairy Man) created people. Other Tule stories describe the creature living in the mountains and stealing food. They say it is still living in remote parts of the area to this day.

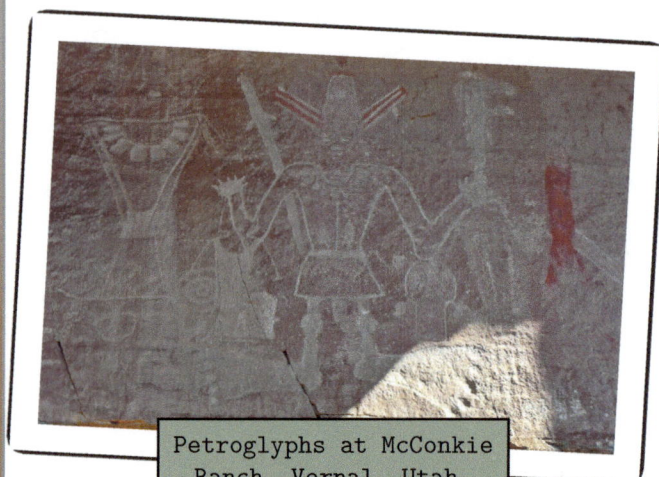

Petroglyphs at McConkie Ranch, Vernal, Utah.

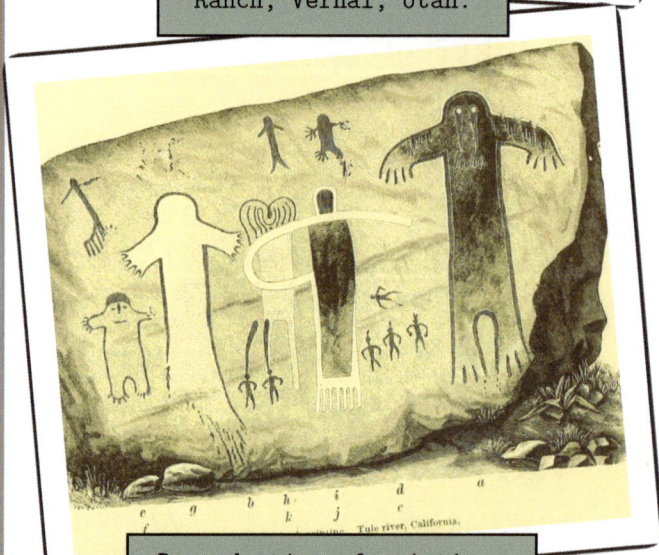

Reproduction of paintings on the Mayak Datat

According to storyteller Roger Fernandes of the Upper S'Kllalam tribe, located in what is now Northwest Washington State, stories about creatures like Bigfoot can have deep meaning for native peoples. "At one level it's just describing what is — there are beings out there living

8

in the forest and they don't associate with us on a regular basis, they are secretive and hide. Another level, mythologically, there are powers in the forest we humans will never truly understand, and maybe these beings represent that power." Overall, then, are these Native stories about Bigfoot supposed to be taken literally? Or are they more about passing along symbols and ideas that help people understand the world around them and themselves?

EUROPEAN TALES

The Europeans who came to the region also would have heard these stories beginning in the 1600s, but increasingly with westward U.S. expansion in the 1800s. They also would also be confronted with things in the forest that they could not explain. Some of the first people to write down histories of these encounters with ape-like creatures were missionaries. For example, Elkanah Walker wrote about Bigfoot in Oregon in 1840: "They come to the people's lodges at night when the people are asleep and take them and put them under their skins and to their place of abode without even waking. Their track is a foot and a half long. They steal salmon from Indian (Native American) nets and eat them raw as the bears do. If the people are awake, they always know when they are coming very near by their strong smell that is most intolerable. It is not uncommon for them to come in the night and give three whistles and then the stones will begin to hit their houses."

Ape Canyon, location of the Battle of Mt. St. Helens

One of the most famous accounts of a Bigfoot sighting was the 1924 Battle of Mt. St. Helens, in which a group of gold prospectors working in Washington State returned to civilization with a story that would capture the public imagination at the time.

The men claimed to have been attacked by enormous, ape-like creatures. According to newspaper reports of the time, the men described the creatures as being around 7 feet (2.1 meters) tall and covered in long, black hair. They recounted a terrifying encounter where the creatures hurled rocks at them and attacked their cabin throughout the night after one of the men shot a rifle at the animals.

The prospectors' story became big local news, but when the U.S. Forest Service sent rangers to investigate, they found no evidence to support the men's story. Even without physical proof, the story became very popular. It made people think of existing folklore about "mountain devils" spoken of by some Native American tribes in the area. As the prospectors' tale was retold and embellished over the years, it became a famous part of the ever-growing legend of Bigfoot.

The most famous account of all, though, came in 1967. In the bright midday sun of the Northern California wilderness, two men were riding horses next to a small creek. As they approached a large tree that had been turned over by a flood, they saw something extraordinary: a large, hairy creature standing at least six feet (1.8 meters) tall, crouching by the stream. One pulled out a video camera and began recording as they jumped off their horses and started running towards what they saw. The men were close to it—no more than 25 feet (7.6 meters) away—when the animal began to walk quickly away, its large, strong arms swinging by its side.

Just before it disappeared into the forest, it turned and looked at the men, giving us the well-known Bigfoot image everybody knows today. For many years, these two men, Roger Patterson and Bob Gimlin, claimed that their minute-long film proved once-and-for-all the existence of this long lost ape-man. The film also inspired generations of believers who are still searching for Bigfoot

Still from the Patterson-Gilman film

to this day. Others insist that the film was a hoax: that the images show nothing more than a tall man in a gorilla costume running around the woods. They claim that Patterson and Gimlin made up the whole thing to get rich and famous. Still, though, the legacy of this encounter is undoubtable: ask most people to think of Bigfoot and they will picture the creature seen in this video.

SCIENTISTS AND SKEPTICS

So while it is clear that Bigfoot has an important place in the culture of many Native Americans and others, especially in the Pacific Northwest, what do the "facts" tell us? What do historians, scientists, archaeologists, and other professionals think about Sasquatch? Do they believe it is—or was—real? The short answer is: "No." Most will point to a lack of evidence, whether fossils or simply bodies of any dead Bigfoot. If they are real, why can no one hold a piece of them in their hands? Some believers will say that there are simply too few of them, in too large and wild an area, for their bodies to be found. Furthermore, the areas in which they are most often "spotted" are temperate rainforests, and the conditions there make fur, skin, and bones deteriorate rapidly. This means that when an animal dies there, its body will quickly return to the earth, and not leave bones to be found later, as opposed to other, drier climates.

This terrain is also another reason cited by believers for why there are so few sightings of Bigfoot, and why the pictures, videos, and sound recordings that do exist are not very convincing. Remember, until fairly recently people did not all have high-quality cameras in their pockets at all times. Most people who went into the areas where Sasquatch are said to live were usually there to do a job, like logging or mining, and would not be carrying the large, expensive cameras of the time. Perhaps we will soon see more evidence of these creatures now because of advances in technology, such as in smartphones and drones. At the same time, though, new artificial intelligence (AI) software might make people skeptical that the images and videos they see—real or not—are fake.

Speaking of newer technologies, today DNA analysis is widely used and trusted. Surely this process could tell us if Sasquatch was its own species, or if it is related to other animals, such as apes, monkeys, or humans? While there have been claims of people being able to extract Bigfoot DNA in the past, most scientists view them with

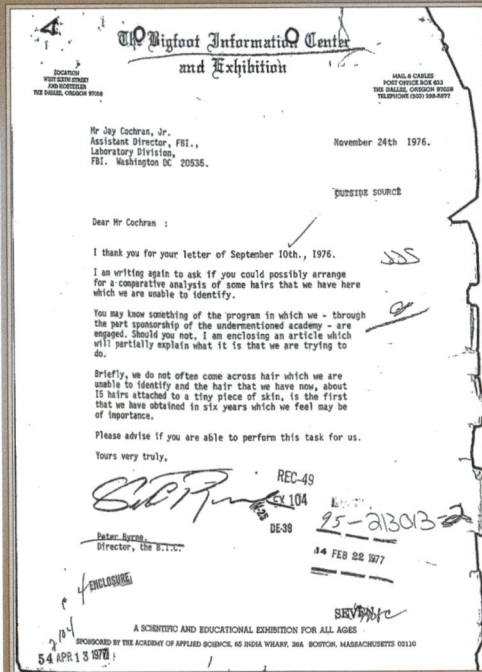

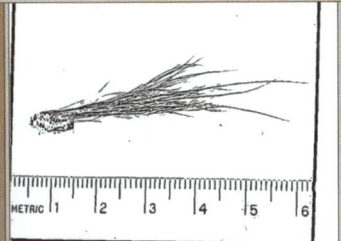

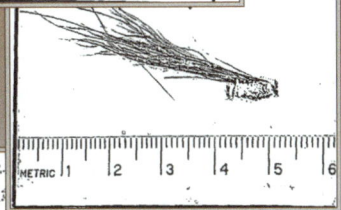

Part of correspondence with the FBI requesting analysis of hairs believed to belong to Bigfoot. Analysis shows they were deer hair.

skepticism. For example, some claimed samples were Bigfoot DNA, but further analysis revealed they belonged to common animals like raccoons or bears.

What about the footprints, though? Clearly, the English name Bigfoot tells us that people must have seen tracks of a very large size, and often enough to make the name stick. In fact, all of the cases mentioned earlier from European sources—the missionary, miners, and two men on horseback—contain references to the beast's footprints. What else could have made these giant impressions in the ground? One way that believers counter skeptics around the topic of footprints is the sheer number and consistency of reports. They argue that misidentification or hoaxes cannot account for all the sightings, and that the footprints themselves offer a unique type of evidence. Many footprint casts have been documented over the years, some measuring up to 16 inches long and 8 inches wide (40x20 centimeters). These footprints are far larger than those of any known animal in North America. However, skeptics argue that misidentified tracks of known animals, perhaps bears walking on their hind legs, could explain some sightings. They also point out that hoaxers have been known to create fake footprints in the past for fun, fame, or just mischief.

Beyond footprints, believers point to other evidence to counter skepticism. Some argue that the blurry nature of many videos and pictures reflects the difficulty of getting a clear shot of a large, elusive creature in its natural habitat. Additionally, believers point to the consistency of descriptions from eyewitnesses across vast stretches of time and geography. These descriptions often include similar details about the creature's size, bipedalism, fur color, and foul odor. Skeptics counter that such similarities could be due to the spread of stories and folklore, rather than representing an actual creature.

THE SEARCHERS

Throughout time, for most people who believed in Bigfoot the main goal was to avoid it, and to keep it away from people, animals, and crops. However, beginning around the middle of the 20th century, there emerged a new group of people: Bigfoot hunters. While it is debatable whether most Native American stories about Bigfoot are meant to be taken literally, the people who look for Bigfoot these days believe in an actual, flesh-and-blood being. Many will go to great—even obsessive—lengths to prove that it exists. Modern Bigfoot hunters range from enthusiastic weekend warriors to researchers with advanced degrees. Amateur groups,

Alleged Bigfoot footprint

Potential Bigfoot sighting

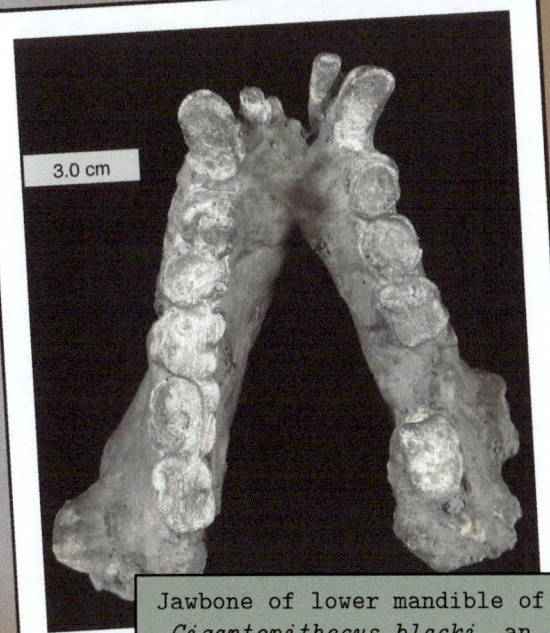
Jawbone of lower mandible of *Gigantopithecus blacki*, an extinct ape

like the Bigfoot Field Researchers Organization (BFRO), organize expeditions, share plaster casts of footprints, and carefully analyze blurry trail camera footage. These citizen scientists are very excited to study Bigfoot but lack the formal training of professional scientists. This can lead to unreliable data or incorrect conclusions. They often rely on their own experience and local knowledge to navigate remote areas and collect data like sound recordings and soil samples.

On the more academic side, researchers, universities, or organizations like the Bigfoot Research Institute (BRI), employ a more scientific approach. They may use DNA analysis, habitat studies, and high-quality recording equipment in their quests for Bigfoot. Annual conferences around the U.S and Canada also bring together researchers, enthusiasts—and even skeptics—to share findings, debate theories, and fuel the ongoing search for Bigfoot.

THE MEDIA

Bigfoot's footprint in popular culture is undeniable. Numerous documentaries introduce viewers to the world of Bigfoot hunters and the blurry evidence they chase. Hollywood has capitalized on the mystery as well, with movies like *Harry and the Hendersons* portraying Bigfoot as a goofy, misunderstood creature. Other movies like *The Legend of Boggy Creek* play up the horror aspect. For many (in North America, especially), television shows like *Finding Bigfoot* have taken center stage, transforming the hunt for Bigfoot into reality TV. These shows follow exciting teams of researchers venturing into the wilderness, armed with thermal cameras and audio recording equipment. While entertainment value is a priority, the shows occasionally present some intriguing evidence, like unusual sound recordings or footprint casts, keeping viewers hooked and convinced that Bigfoot might appear after the next commercial break. Popular culture ensures Bigfoot remains a topic of conversation for many, but it can also distort public perception. Some portrayals turn the mischievous and elusive creature of Native myth into a monstrous threat. They can also blur the line between folklore and fact, and cheapen both the cultural and scientific aspects.

CONCLUSION?

The legend of Bigfoot remains an exciting mystery for both believers and skeptics. Believers claim to have many pieces of evidence: massive footprints exceeding known animal sizes, blurry videos capturing fleeting

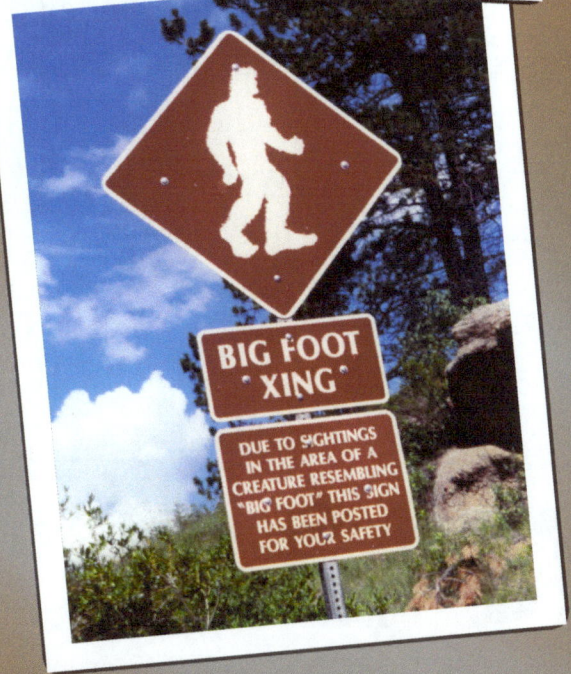

glimpses, and consistent descriptions from witnesses across vast areas. However, skeptics counter that the lack of verifiable physical evidence like fossils or DNA creates too much doubt. They argue, for example, that blurry footage and footprint casts could be hoaxes or misidentified animal tracks.

The search for Bigfoot continues, fueled by a mix of scientific curiosity and amateur enthusiasm. Modern Bigfoot hunters roam the forests, while the media also plays a large role in keeping the myth alive and even evolving it, with documentaries, movies, and reality TV shows introducing Bigfoot to a wider audience. While these portrayals can be entertaining, they can also exaggerate the creature's characteristics and mislead the public.

Ultimately, the question of Bigfoot's existence remains an open debate. The evidence is far from conclusive, but the enduring mystery continues to capture imaginations and inspire exploration. Whether Bigfoot is a real creature or a product of folklore, the legend serves as a reminder of the vast unknowns that may still exist in the world around us. Will future advancements in science and technology shed light on this mystery? Or will Bigfoot forever remain a captivating enigma? The answer may await those who are willing to delve deeper.

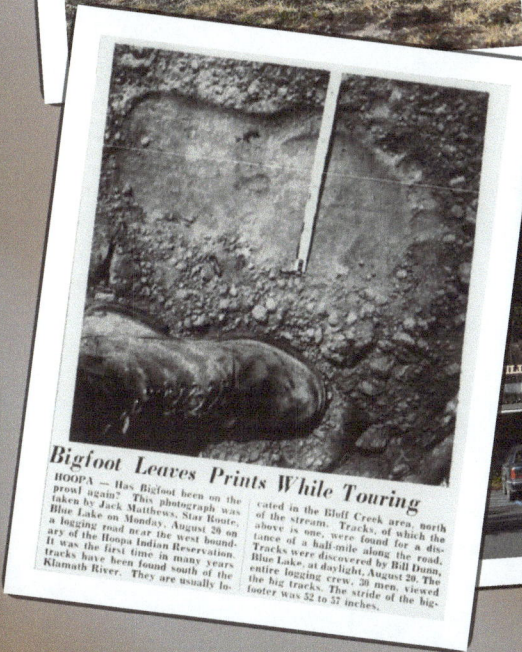

Bigfoot Leaves Prints While Touring

HOOPA — Has Bigfoot been on the prowl again? This photograph was taken by Jack Matthews, Star Route, Blue Lake on Monday, August 20 on a logging road near the west boundary of the Hoopa Indian Reservation. It was the first time in many years tracks have been found south of the Klamath River. They are usually located in the Bluff Creek area, north of the stream. Tracks, of which the above is one, were found for a distance of a half-mile along the road. Tracks were discovered by Bill Dunn, Blue Lake, at daylight, August 20. The entire logging crew, 30 men, viewed the big tracks. The stride of the big footer was 52 to 57 inches.

LEARN MORE

"Bigfoot: Is the Sasquatch Real?", Live Science:
https://www.livescience.com/24598-bigfoot.html

"New Exhibit Showcases Sasquatch Through Native Perspectives" Tulalip News:
https://www.tulalipnews.com/2018/07/12/new-exhibit-showcases-sasquatch-through-native-perspectives

THE THEORIES

1. Bigfoot was real, but is now extinct.

Evidence: This would explain the many stories passed down through the generations by native peoples and even by more modern accounts, depending on when you think it went extinct.

This could be the reason that today, even with many more people searching for Bigfoot, and with modern technology, there's no concrete evidence.

Counter-evidence: But why are there no fossils—or other evidence that we can touch—to prove this? We have dinosaur bones from millions of years ago, after all!

There may be many legends that can be read as "Bigfoot Stories", but are they really all that similar? As we know, all cultures pass down accounts of monsters, so how do we know these are all about the same creature?

2. Bigfoot is not real, and the stories have all been made up for various reasons.

Evidence: All ancient cultures (and even many modern ones) tell scary stories about strange and unexplained creatures. The legend of Bigfoot is simply another example of this.

People today have reasons to lie about seeing Bigfoot or finding traces of it. They can make a lot of money or become popular on social media or on TV by saying these things.

Counter-evidence: But what about all the similarities in the stories passed down from the people who first came to the American continent? These people did not all speak the same language and also often lived far apart, both in time and space. However, the stories all have many similarities. What explains this?

There are plenty of people who say they have found evidence of Bigfoot but do not try to profit off of it. In addition, there are also some scientists and other smart people who think Bigfoot is real. Why would they be lying?

3. Bigfoot is real, but is an endangered species and good at hiding, so they are rarely seen.

Evidence: There have been many animal species discovered only recently, as the word is a vast and often unknown place. Who is to say that this isn't also true of Bigfoot?

Until recently, most people did not know that dinosaurs ruled the planet for millions of years. Even after the fossils began to be discovered, people continued to deny that dinosaurs were real. Perhaps this will prove true for Bigfoot as well.

Counter-evidence: Even if Bigfoot was good at hiding, nearly everyone alive today has a good camera in their pocket at all times. In addition, technology as a whole is so advanced that no species could really hide if people wanted to find it enough.

If Bigfoot were real, wouldn't governments all be competing to find it and try to use it as a weapon, to train as a "super-soldier"? Could it really be possible that no country could have captured one?

WHY DOES IT MATTER?

Seeking knowledge exploring the unknown are key features of humans, and have helped us to make exceptional progress as a species, both in culture and technology. How does the search for Bigfoot fit into this aspect of humanity? Some might argue that with so much change and technological advancement today, chasing Bigfoot is a way to go back to a more simple time of legends and monsters. After all, isn't one of the most basic human emotions fear, and specifically fear of the unknown? By proving (or disproving) the existence of Bigfoot, people may be trying to take back some control that they feel they've lost in their society and in their own lives.

As a part of the folklore of many of the native people of North America, stories about Bigfoot, or Sasquatch, can help us understand more about their history and beliefs. Are you interested in reading more stories like this and learning more about these cultures now? While this story is very exciting, there are thousands more that these cultures used (and still use) to describe and interpret the world around them. Can you think of any similar stories from your country or culture? It may be interesting to compare and contrast them with the story of Bigfoot.

Many people today feel like they can't trust what they're told by people in power, like scientists, politicians, and the news media. Some people think that the government or other groups are hiding the truth about Bigfoot, which has made a lot of people look for answers in other places. Has this feeling of distrust has made the search for Bigfoot even more popular? It may well be that Bigfoot is a special case, and that most of the people who claim to believe it really do. But it may also be about just saying "no" to what people who are supposed to be experts are telling you that makes Bigfoot truthers (and others) enjoy it so much.

All the talk about Bigfoot helps people think more about environmental conservation and endangered species. Does learning about this topic make you want to get out into the wilderness? While many Bigfoot hunters grew up in and around the forests where the creature is said to live, others have gotten in touch with nature for the first time through this pursuit. In the end, could searching for Bigfoot and other creatures help get more people into environmentalism? If so, that may be a good enough reason for people to practice this hobby.

FUN FACTS

Bigfoot with Legal Protection? Believe It or Not! Skamania County, Washington, holds a unique place in Bigfoot history. In 1969, they passed a law making it illegal to kill Bigfoot. Originally intended as a lighthearted response to the growing Bigfoot craze, the law still stands today.

Bigfoot Apps! There's an app for (almost) everything these days, and Bigfoot is no exception. From Bigfoot footprint identifiers to "calls of the wild" sound generators (meant to attract Bigfoot!), these apps cater to the Bigfoot enthusiast and maybe even hope to capture some real-time evidence.

Bigfoot on Patrol? Park rangers in Mount St. Helens National Park used to jokingly tell visitors that they needed a Bigfoot permit to go hiking. While it was all in good fun, it highlights the enduring presence of Bigfoot in the cultural consciousness of the Pacific Northwest.

GLOSSARY

arachaeologist (n.) — Scientists who study the history and culture of ancient people by digging up their remains.

bipedalism (n.) — The way of moving by using two feet, like humans do.

branched off (v.) — Separated from a larger group and becoming different over time.

cryptid (n.) — An animal that is rumored to exist but has never been proven real.

deteriorate (v.) — To decay or rot over time.

elusive (adj.) — Difficult to find or catch.

embellished (v.) — Added extra details that are not necessarily true to a story, often to make it more exciting.

etched (v.) — Carved or scratched a design onto a surface.

folklore (n.) — Traditional stories, beliefs, and customs passed down through generations by word of mouth.

legacy (n.) — Something that is left behind from the past.

missionary (n.) — A person who travels to spread a religion.

mischievous (adj.) someone who likes to cause trouble in a playful way.

Native American (n.) — The original people of North and South America.

Neanderthal (n.) — An extinct human species related to modern humans.

pictograph (n.) — Drawings or symbols painted on rock surfaces.

prospector (n.) — People who search for gold or other valuable minerals.

sheer (adj.) — Very great or large in amount or degree.

sightings (n. pl.) — The act of seeing something, especially something unusual.

skeptic (n.) — A person who doubts something is true. They want to see convincing evidence before they will believe it.

terrain (n.) — The features of a land area, such as mountains, rivers, and forests.

tracks (n. pl.) — The marks left by an animal or person walking, running, or crawling.

DISCUSSION QUESTIONS

1. **The Legacy of Bigfoot**: Stories of Bigfoot have been around for centuries. Why do you think these stories persist even though there's no scientific proof of Bigfoot's existence? What do these stories tell us about the places where they are told?

2. **Seeing is Believing?**: Eyewitness accounts are a big part of the Bigfoot mystery. Why do you think so many people believe they've seen Bigfoot? Do you think any of the sightings are misidentification or hoaxes? What kind of evidence would be convincing proof of Bigfoot's existence?

3. **Science vs. Folklore**: Bigfoot research relies on both scientific methods like DNA analysis and footprint casting, as well as folklore and traditions. How can these two seemingly different approaches work together in the search for Bigfoot? Are there other mysteries where science and folklore might intersect?

4. **The Thrill of the Hunt**: Many people are drawn to the idea of searching for Bigfoot. What is the appeal of searching for something that might not even exist? What other unexplained creatures or mysteries capture people's imaginations?

5. **Protecting the Unknown**: If Bigfoot were real, how would humans and Bigfoot interact? Should we protect Bigfoot as an endangered species, or would it be a threat to humans? Why or why not?

PROJECTS

1. **Non-Fiction Essay** Choose one of the following positions and write a persuasive essay with the title "Fact or Fiction? Examining the Evidence for Bigfoot."
   - **Argue for** the existence of Bigfoot based on compelling evidence (eyewitness accounts, footprint casts, etc.) and propose next steps for research
   - **Argue against** the existence of Bigfoot, explaining weaknesses in the evidence and alternative explanations for sightings.

2. **Fiction Project:** Choose a prompt or make up one of your own.
   - Write a diary entry from the perspective of a young researcher who spends a summer searching for Bigfoot.
   - Create a fictional news report about the capture of a Bigfoot creature, exploring the scientific and social implications.
   - Write a short story set in a world where Bigfoot coexists with humans, exploring the challenges and opportunities of this relationship.

3. **Research Project**: Choose a topic from below.
   - **Topic 1**: Deep dive into a specific aspect of Bigfoot research, such as footprint analysis, DNA testing, or Native American folklore surrounding Bigfoot.
   - **Topic 2:** Research other cryptids around the world and compare/contrast them with Bigfoot.
   - **Topic 3**: Investigate the history of hoaxes in Bigfoot research and how they've impacted the search for the creature.

4. **Butterfly Effect:** Imagine that humans found proof that Bigfoot is 100% real some time in the past. What would that look like? How would events in history (and up to today and into the future) have changed? Describe when, where, and how humans got this proof, and then create an (alternate) historical timeline from then until now that has important events in Bigfoot/human history.

REFERENCES

Britannica, T. Editors of Encyclopaedia (2024, July 1). "Sasquatch." *Encyclopedia Britannica*.

"Bigfoot (Sasquatch) Legend", Oregon Encyclopedia: "Bigfoot: Is the Sasquatch Real?" Live Science: https://www.livescience.com/24598-bigfoot.html

Datat, M. (2022). "The Hairy Man Pictographs". *Relict Hominid Inquiry*, 1(12), 1-12. https://www.isu.edu/media/libraries/rhi/research-papers/Mayak-Datat-Hairy-Man-Pictographs-1.pdf

Harper, E. (2024, March 12). "Native American Bigfoot Legends and Lore." *Hangar1publishing*. https://hangar1publishing.com/blogs/cryptids/native-american-bigfoot

Kalliber, K. (2018, July 12). "New Exhibit Showcases Sasquatch Through Native Perspectives." *Tulalip News*. https://www.tulalipnews.com/2018/07/12/new-exhibit-showcases-sasquatch-through-native-perspectives/

"New Exhibit Showcases Sasquatch Through Native Perspectives", Tulalip News: https://www.tulalipnews.com/2018/07/12/new-exhibit-showcases-sasquatch-through-native-perspectives

Perry, D. (2018, January 25). How a 1924 Bigfoot Battle Helped Launch a Northwest Legend. Oregonlive. https://www.oregonlive.com/history/2018/01/1924_bigfoot_battle_on_mt_st_h.html#:~:text=flank%20of%20Mt.-,St

Pester, P. (2022, November 16). "Bigfoot: Is the Sasquatch Real?" Livescience.com. https://www.livescience.com/24598-bigfoot.html

Roos, D. (2023, July 14). How Early Humans First Reached the Americas: 3 Theories. HISTORY. https://www.history.com/news/human-migration-americas-beringia

Walls, R. (2022, September 7). "Bigfoot (Sasquatch) Legend. "*The Oregon Encyclopedia*. https://www.oregonencyclopedia.org/articles/bigfoot_sasquatch_legend/

Z. (2021, March 29). Common Thread Series: Rock-Throwing. Apes of the Uncanny Valley. https://apesoftheuncannyvalley.wordpress.com/2021/03/29/common-thread-series-rock-throwing/

ISBN: 978-1-956159-57-8 (print)

For permission requests, write to the publisher at "ATTN: Permissions", at the address below:

29 Milo Dr. Branford, CT 06405 USA
info@alphabetpublishingbooks.com
www.AlphabetPublishingBooks.com

Discounts on class sets and bulk orders available upon inquiry.

Cover and Interior Design by Walton Burns

Country of Manufacture Specified on Last Page

First Printing 2025

Images

www.ingramcontent.com/pod-product-compliance
Lightning Source LLC
Chambersburg PA
CBHW061147030426
42335CB00002B/131